When Whales CROSS the SEA

THE GRAY WHALE MIGRATION

by Sharon Katz Cooper

illustrated by Tom Leonard

PICTURE WINDOW BOOKS
a capstone imprint

Thanks to our advisers for their expertise, research, and advice:

Diane Alps, Marine Mammal Biologist
Cabrillo Marine Aquarium, San Pedro, California

Terry Flaherty, PhD, Professor of English
Minnesota State University, Mankato

Editor: Jill Kalz
Designer: Lori Bye
Art Director: Nathan Gassman
Production Specialist: Laura Manthe
The illustrations in this book were created with acrylics.
Image Credit: XNR Productions, 3 (map)

Picture Window Books are published by Capstone,
1710 Roe Crest Drive, North Mankato, Minnesota 56003
www.capstonepub.com

Library of Congress Cataloging-in-Publication Data
Katz Cooper, Sharon, author.
  When whales cross the sea : the gray whale migration / by Sharon Katz
Cooper, illustrated by Tom Leonard.
     pages cm. — (Nonfiction picture books. Extraordinary migrations)
  Summary: "Follows a single gray whale on its annual migration
journey"—Provided by publisher.
  Audience: K to grade 3.
  Includes bibliographical references and index.
  ISBN 978-1-4795-6079-0 (library binding)
  ISBN 978-1-4795-6107-0 (paper over board)
  ISBN 978-1-4795-6103-2 (paperback)
  ISBN 978-1-4795-6111-7 (eBook PDF)
1. Gray whale—Behavior—Juvenile literature. 2. Animal migration—
Juvenile literature. I. Leonard, Thomas, 1955– illustrator.
II. Title. III. Title: Gray whale migration.
  QL737.C425K38 2015
  599.5'22—dc23   2014024416

Each year gray whales make one of the longest migrations of any mammal in the world. They swim 5,000 to 7,000 miles (8,050 to 11,265 kilometers) from their summer homes to warm winter waters. Swimming nearly 100 miles (160 km) per day, they make the trip in two to three months. Why travel so far?

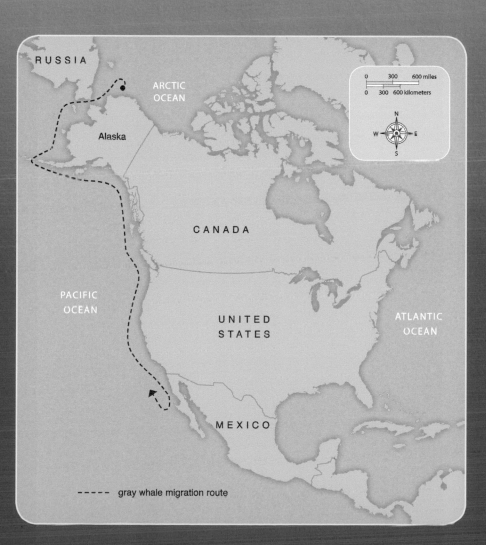

RUSSIA

ARCTIC OCEAN

Alaska

CANADA

PACIFIC OCEAN

UNITED STATES

ATLANTIC OCEAN

MEXICO

0   300   600 miles
0   300   600 kilometers

N
W   E
S

- - - - - gray whale migration route

Bump ... SWISH! The whale hits the edge of a large ice chunk. She's done that three times already this week.

It is October in the Arctic, and patches of ice are growing larger. Days are getting shorter. Waters are getting colder. Feeding season is almost done. The whale knows it's time to start heading south, to the warmer waters of Mexico. She has something very important to do there.

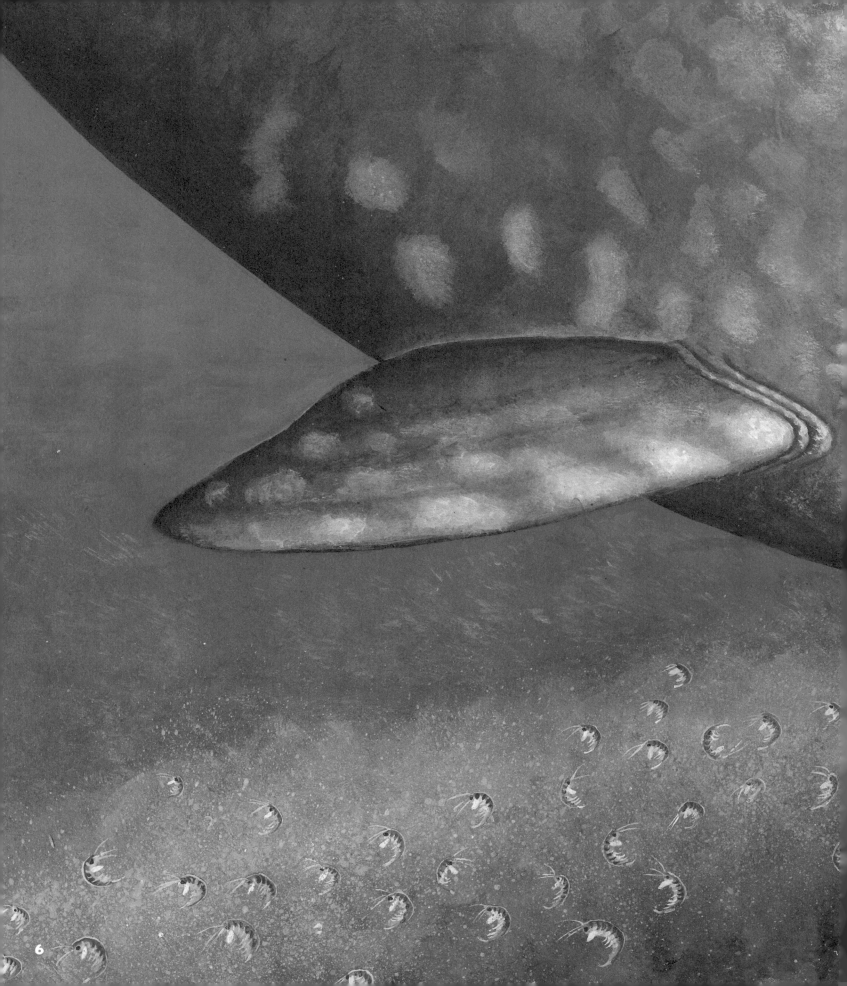

The whale feeds for a few more days. She eats almost non-stop—about 1.2 tons (1.1 metric tons) of tiny shrimplike animals each day. All that food weighs about as much as a small car! The whale weighs 40 tons (36 t) herself, though. That's as much as 33 small cars.

The whale leaves the Arctic and swims south along the coast. She has a full belly and a thick layer of blubber covering her body. The fat layer is just what she needs. It's like a coat and a restaurant in one. The blubber keeps the whale warm and gives her energy.

The whale swims with power through the ocean. She stays close to the shore, where the water is shallower. Shallow water means less chance of meeting a hungry orca.

She peeks her head above water. Landmarks on shore help her find her way.

During the journey the whale slows down to rest, but she never stops. She doesn't even eat. She must get to her winter home on time. A warm coastal lagoon awaits her. There's no time to waste.

Finally, after about 60 days, the whale's journey ends—just in time too! She's having a baby! A healthy, 1,000-pound (454-kilogram) baby whale.

The baby whale must grow quickly. In a few months, he will join his mother for the long journey back north. He does not have a thick layer of blubber yet. The waters of the lagoon keep him warm while he is still small.

The lagoon is safe from orcas. But it doesn't have a lot of food. To help him grow, the mother whale feeds her baby 50 gallons (189 liters) of milk every day. He can gain up to 60 pounds (27 kg) each day! At the same time, the mother whale loses a lot of blubber. She does not eat much and puts her energy into making milk.

The mother whale helps her baby to swim. She shows him how to plow up the seafloor to look for food. He will need to do this when they reach their summer home in the Arctic.

After three months it is time to start the long, challenging trip north. There are many dangers on this journey, including orcas, large ships, and polluted waters.

Good luck on your journey, whales. Be safe, and see you next year!

Gray Whale Fast Facts

Scientific name: *Eschrichtius robustus*

Type of whale: baleen (filters food through a comblike structure called baleen, rather than using teeth)

Full-grown weight: 40–45 tons (36–41 metric tons)

Weight at birth: 1,000–1,500 pounds (454–680 kilograms)

Whale milk: very thick and rich; 53-percent fat (human milk is about 2-percent fat)

Nursing: young whales drink their mother's milk for 7 to 9 months

Diet: amphipods and tube worms from the ocean floor; gray whales are the only whales that are bottom feeders

Blubber layer: 6–10 inches (15–25 centimeters)

Life span: 60 years or more

Predators: orcas and humans

Total length of migration: 10,000 to 14,000 miles (16,100 to 22,500 kilometers) round-trip

Critical Thinking Using the Common Core

1. Why can't gray whales stay in the waters of the Arctic Ocean year-round? Why do they migrate south? (Key Ideas and Details)

2. Describe how the mother whale takes care of her baby in the lagoon. (Key Ideas and Details)

3. Look at the map on page 3. What does the dotted line show? (Craft and Structure)

Glossary

amphipod—a small shrimplike animal

blubber—a thick layer of fat under the skin of some animals

coastal lagoon—a large, shallow body of water protected from the ocean by barrier islands

landmark—something that stands out, such as a big tree or a building

mammal—a warm-blooded animal that breathes air; mammals have hair or fur; female mammals give birth to live young and feed them milk

migration—the movement from one area to another on a regular basis, usually to find food or to produce young

orca—a kind of whale that's black and white; also called a killer whale, the ocean's top predator

polluted—dirty and harmful to living things

predator—an animal that hunts other animals for food

Read More

Catt, Thessaly. *Migrating with the Humpback Whale.* Animal Journeys. New York: PowerKids Press, 2011.

Cohn, Scotti. *On the Move: Seasonal Migrations.* Mt. Pleasant, S.C.: Sylvan Dell Publishing, 2013.

Gunderson, Megan M. *Gray Whales.* Whales. Set 1. Edina, Minn.: ABDO Pub., 2011.

Sayre, April Pulley. *Here Come the Humpbacks!* Watertown, Mass.: Charlesbridge, 2013.

Internet Sites

FactHound offers a safe, fun way to find Internet sites related to this book. All of the sites on FactHound have been researched by our staff.

Here's all you do:

Visit *www.facthound.com*

Type in this code: 9781479560790

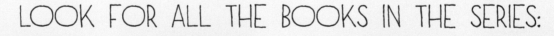

Check out projects, games and lots more at
www.capstonekids.com

Index

LOOK FOR ALL THE BOOKS IN THE SERIES: